HOME SERIES

HOME SERIES
LIVING WITH COLOUR

BETA-PLUS

CONTENTS

9   Foreword

14   Muted and chic colours for a city apartment
20   Vibrant colours in a historic castle
24   The colourful decor of Bistro de la Mer
28   A combination of classic design and contemporary art
36   The exemplary restoration of a village home
42   A warm palette of colours
46   A distinctive loft for an art-lover
52   Nostalgic and poetic
58   Coming home
66   Rooms with a view
68   Strong contrasts in a cosy apartment
70   Grandeur and intimacy
76   Artistic inspiration in an 18th-century farmhouse
82   A contemporary lifestyle in an old setting
88   A sophisticated country house
96   The authenticity of lime paints
100   Transforming a cellar into a relaxation room
106   A dialogue between ethnic inspiration and contemporary art and design
112   A symphony in white in an ancient castle
118   Contemporary style for a Normandy-inspired villa

P. 4-5
Farrow & Ball, the British manufacturer of traditional paints, has developed a range of over 100 shades, formulated after years of painstaking research.

P. 6
This interior by Christine Bekaert is in a warm red shade to which iron oxide has been added. A self-portrait by Andy Warhol.

FOREWORD

 olour is a universal language and a way of expressing ourselves. It is one of the most important elements for bringing atmosphere and character into a home.

Colours have many different associations and virtues: they can calm and relax us or make us feel energised. However, colours are often difficult to choose and may not always be simple to combine. Using a basic palette of three primary colours, with the addition of black and white, you can create an endless range of different shades: muted, vibrant, saturated or subdued.

Our subjective experience of colour, constantly changing fashions and a great diversity of colour ranges are a theme running through the long history of interior architecture.

All of the projects presented in this book were created by experts in contemporary interior design throughout western Europe. The selected colour palettes all owe something to local architectural traditions and to the style of the property.

Subtle, monochrome colours set the tone in many of the projects. Opting for a sober, minimalist style also has an influence on the use of colour.

Other interiors feature a slightly more exuberant take on colour, with a rich and varied palette showing influences from all over the world.

Whether the colour scheme is white, minimalist or brightly coloured, one theme runs through this book: the consistent use of traditional paints of the highest quality. Particular attention is also devoted to the application of the colour. Experts with great respect for tradition demonstrate their skill and craftsmanship, passed down through the generations and immortalised in amazing projects with a perfect finish.

P. 8
Antiques dealer Axel Vervoordt has installed part of his collection in a restored malt house. The selection of colours creates a special atmosphere in every room of this amazing building.

P. 10-11
The walls of this country house are in natural pigments: the patina of the bookshelves was achieved using traditional, time-honoured techniques.

MUTED AND CHIC COLOURS

FOR A CITY APARTMENT

T his project features a unique city apartment of 185m².

The young owners asked interior architects Ensemble & Associés to design a cosy home in warm and muted shades.

The result was a modern, contemporary look, where colour serves to structure the space.

The living room opens onto the kitchen on one side and onto a corridor leading to the bedrooms on the other side. Nuances of grey, beige and taupe combined with a touch of orange. The shelves are in beveka walnut wood. Van Caster carpet. Furniture by Luz Interiors.

A more dramatic colour in the entrance hall: a vermilion wall with a family portrait. The adjacent guest toilet has a composite stone surface, taps by Dornbracht, an Alape washbasin and units in fitted beveka walnut wood.

The shelving unit forms the central axis in the apartment. It is a custom-built design by Ensemble & Associés, in beveka walnut wood.

P. 17-19
Streamlined contemporary
furniture by Luz Interiors.

VIBRANT COLOURS

IN A HISTORIC CASTLE

D ating back to the early thirteenth century, Castle Rameyenhof assumed its final form in around 1550. Restoration work has recently been completed.

The Dutch interior designer Claartje de Gruyter lives in these unique surroundings, where she displays her fondness for unusual combinations of timeless objects and works of art from a wide variety of cultures.

A beautiful mix of old objects in a warm, colourful home.

The interior designer's personal taste is the theme running through this project: simple and sober, authentic in the choice of furniture and the colour scheme.

THE COLOURFUL DECOR

OF BISTRO DE LA MER

D ominique Koch is a talented interior designer who has managed various restoration projects on the Belgian coast.

All of her projects feature her individual use of colour in timeless settings.

A well-known restaurateur contacted Dominique Koch with a special project: to modernise the interior of his restaurant to create a trend-setting bistro in a contemporary marine style.

The designer had carte blanche for this project. Her only instruction was to work with shades of white and blue, a request that Dominique Koch interpreted extremely loosely, as can be seen from the photographs in this report.

Her response was to evoke a maritime atmosphere through the selection of furniture and decorative objects, but in a completely new, warmer colour palette.

The association of dark red and chocolate brown is equally attractive in the evening and during the daytime. The designer used matte colours to achieve the right effect. Koch found the old fishing lines in junk shops in coastal villages.

Dominique Koch's creative approach achieved a convincing result, in spite of the limited budget. Around the bar, shelves made from old planks. The floor is in a seagrass carpet: tough, timeless and hygienic.

The Vichy tablecloths and the many maritime objects create the atmosphere of an authentic fishermen's café.

A COMBINATION OF CLASSIC DESIGN

AND CONTEMPORARY ART

T his apartment, decorated in a contemporary classic style by RR Interieur, has an atmosphere of discreet luxury.

This project features a harmonious combination of designer elements and contemporary art.

This sober colour palette with subtle nuances of beige, grey and black shows the furniture to its best advantage.

Vermilion lends a lively touch to the colour scheme.

P. 28-31
Leather sofa by Minotti and a specially made carpet.
Cab chairs around a wooden table, which was also custom-made for this project.

A sober, minimalist atmosphere in this bedroom in black and white. A comfortable bed with bedclothes from RR Interieur.

The second bedroom in this seaside apartment.

THE EXEMPLARY RESTORATION

OF A VILLAGE HOME

T his picturesque home has been restored by the former owners of Kasimir's Antique Studio, with a passion for detail and full of respect for the authentic surroundings.

This small house has been completely restored to the way it once was, but a few discreet additions have given it a contemporary touch.

The colour is of the utmost importance and the finish also makes a significant contribution to the decorative effect. The lime paints, applied using traditional methods, create an authentic atmosphere.

All of the walls were painted with Corical lime paints. The hand-made tiles are from Dominique Desimpel.

These hand-made tiles in ox-blood red lend a touch of warmth to the apartment.

A look that is both timeless and
contemporary, with sisal on the floor
and a cosy chair.

A WARM PALETTE OF COLOURS

Architect Bernard De Clerck takes a global view of all of his projects: the design and construction (or renovation) of a house are closely connected to the furnishings and decoration.

His architectural studio does not only design the house, but often also manages the finish of the property, in collaboration with painters, fabric workshops and other professionals.

The colours and fabrics selected for these homes play an important part in creating the atmosphere. The architect selects them in consultation with the client and in harmony with the overall design concept.

De Clerck chose a warm colour palette for this project.
Arlette Gesquière finished the fabrics in this report.

The curtain fabric is Morris (plain) by Ian Sanderson.
Firenze voile from Decortex.
Tablecloth in Sparta fabric by Rubelli.

Icaro bedclothes by Vano.

The bed and headboard are in a checked Ripley fabric by Ian Sanderson.

P. 44
Curtain in Lampang silk by Ramm, Son
& Crocker.
A Java sisal carpet by Louis De Poortere
(Vivaldi collection).

A DISTINCTIVE LOFT

FOR AN ART-LOVER

T his distinctive loft was designed by Olivier Dwek's architecture and interiors studio.

Esther Gutmer selected the furniture in harmony with the interior and the owner's extensive collection of art. The space is structured by the interplay of lines and the use of colour: toning shades of red for the chairs and carpet turn this space into a distinct zone.

The dramatic hanging lamp is from Instore (Dome XXL, designed by Ingo Maurer).

P. 47-49
An unusual harmony of red and white in this dining room, office and sitting room.

A typical loft style: the concrete structure is exposed in the bedroom and the mezzanine, which are in the same colour scheme as the rest of the apartment (red, white and black).

NOSTALGIC AND POETIC

« I do not like new houses: the sight of them leaves me cold. » This quote from Sully Prudhomme in *Les Solitudes* adorns the front of interior designer Dominique Koch's address book.

It is a perfect illustration of her passion for old houses that have been restored with respect for their authenticity and timeless atmosphere.

Dominique Koch restored her own house and oversees around a dozen interior projects every year, which have a common theme: they all display her nostalgic vision and her respect for the past and for traditional craftsmanship.

The armchairs are upholstered in a red and saffron-yellow fabric by Bruder. The small checked design is by Brunschwig & Fils.

Un canapé de Vandekerckhove recouvert d'un tissu de Ralph Lauren.

The checked fabric of the blind and cushions is by Tissus Colbert.

A Jules Flipo carpet.

An 18th-century armchair upholstered in rough linen by Bruder.
The other sofas are also in Bruder fabrics: in cotton, linen and cotton/silk.

Blind, sofa upholstery and cushions in
Malabar fabrics by Bruder.

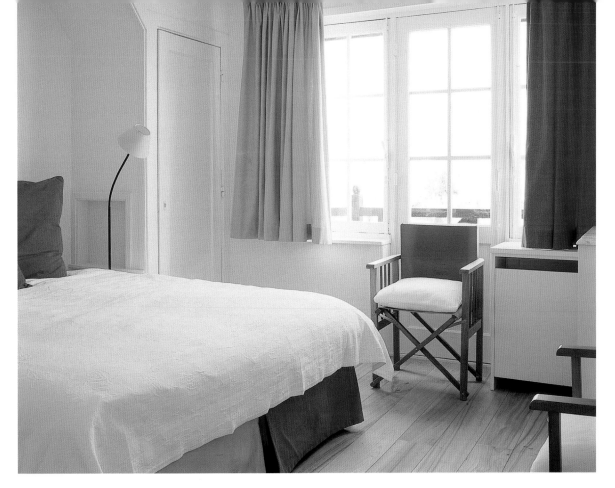

Dominique Koch rents out a house to Marie-Lise Friberg, who comes from Sweden. This Scandinavian-inspired interior has curtains and fabrics by Dominique Koch. A fine example of what can be achieved with simple fabrics (here by Ikea). A decorative effect featuring the primary colours of magenta, cyan and yellow.

The curtains and blinds in this dining room are in an Etamine fabric by Jane Churchill: monochrome for the curtains and a checked design for the blinds.

COMING HOME

T he interiors of renowned designer Walda Pairon all have one thing in common: they offer their owners the ideal space to relax and be themselves.

For Walda, this signifies a constant quest for calm and wellbeing.

The selection of fabrics and colours is of prime importance in her aim to create the highest quality living spaces.

She has applied her principles to great effect in her own home.

The chairs are upholstered in a pale-beige « Collobières » fabric by Pierre Frey.

Blue and purple in this romantic sitting room. Walda Pairon bought an old roll of velour to upholster the armchair and cover the round table.
The violet cushion on the table is in a fabric by Fanny Aronsen. The other purple cushion (left in the photo) is in a Marquis fabric by Sahco Hesslein.

This room also shows the designer's talent, with a few simple decorative elements combined to create an original, sophisticated look. Sisal carpet and an antique kilim made by nomadic Berbers. The armchair is in fabrics by Sahco Hesslein and J. Pansu.

A linen fabric in natural colours and a wool-like yellow silk fabric by Bruder were chosen for the curtains. A tablecloth by Fanny Aronsen. Cushions by Malabar, Romo and Aronsen. The footstool is upholstered in a Romo fabric.

The armchair is in a fabric by Brunschwig & Fils. Velour cushions by J. Pansu and Burger.

Transparent linen by the Italian manufacturer Cortis. The blue cushion is by Fanny Aronsen. The bed is in a Bruder fabric (Malabar collection).

Curtains in a Romo check design. The transparent fabric on the right is by Cortis.

The blue and green fabric for the curtains is by Decortex. The bench is in a velvet fabric by Bragance. A green blind by Malabar.

ROOMS WITH A VIEW

S outh Limburg has always been seen as the Italy of the Netherlands. The region's rolling hills and the cultural atmosphere certainly would not seem out of place in Italy.

Dutch hotelier Camille Oostwegel, assisted by his wife, has developed a small empire of tasteful castle hotels in the beautiful surroundings of Maastricht, restoring ruins, castles, mansions, farmhouses and abbeys to their former glory, always with great affection and a passion for details.

The Oostwegel hotel rooms are often very colourful, as these photographs demonstrate.

Two rooms in bright, dramatic colours in the Winselerhof Hotel.

STRONG CONTRASTS

IN A COSY APARTMENT

Péristyle interior design company, under the direction of Axelle François, created the decoration for this 1964 apartment with a sea view, which was recently renovated.

The result: rich contrasts and daring colour combinations, with shades of red predominating.

A T Line sofa.

Red bed linen from Sèvres.

The chest of drawers, with its carefully cerused finish, is from the Netherlands.

GRANDEUR AND INTIMACY

Themenos interior design studio created this beautiful country house with a respect for natural materials.

The basic materials (wood, brick and stone) have been used for centuries. Here, they have been painted and adapted to modern requirements.

Themenos kept these materials in their most natural form: old Burgundy slabs for the entrance hall and the kitchen; bricks and stones both inside and out, in a beautiful range of colours, in harmony with the earthy shades. Wood has been used to great effect throughout the project. Making effective use of such intense, bright colours over large areas was quite a challenge. The ceilings are painted in the same shades as the walls, further reinforcing the dramatic effect.

An atmosphere of grandeur in this entrance hall, with old Burgundy slabs on the floor. Curtains in hand-coloured cotton. The decor of this entrance hall is emphasised by the warmth of the colour on the walls.

De Waal decorators created a very strong colour palette for this country house, on the basis of Corical lime paints.

The walls are in an amaranth shade by Corical for a warm effect.

In the living room, the wall units are made of long wall panels: a complete L, in brushed oak, with a bleached finish.
The oak planks have a pale-grey finish that accentuates the structure of the wood. A built-in plasma screen and hi-fi are concealed above the fireplace, which has retained its central position.

The floor in aged oak with a dark painted finish creates a contrast between the kitchen and the living room. The windows were painted black, both inside and outside. Dark shades were selected for the curtains and blinds too, resulting in a very warm atmosphere, particularly on winter evenings.

A marble floor for this breakfast corner.

ARTISTIC INSPIRATION

IN AN 18TH-CENTURY FARMHOUSE

A rtist Daan van Doorn applied artistic principles when restoring this eighteenth-century farmhouse, which is a listed monument.

The authentic character of the farmhouse has been retained, but the use of sophisticated shades of grey lends a contemporary touch. Most of the chairs are from the Job Interieur collection.

This alcove provides a new frame for an old-style portrait by Daan van Doorn. A Job sofa.

The entrance hall, with a drawing by Daan van Doorn. The colours throughout the entire house were designed on the basis of the colour pigments that the artist uses in his portraits. All of the colours are his own creations.

P. 78-79
A view of the living room. The doors to the alcove have a Turkish touch: a fertility symbol that the artist has incorporated into his house in various places.

The dining room, with the entrance to the kitchen. On the wall, an oil painting in brown-red shades in perfect harmony with the colour of the tiling.

P. 80
The colourful kitchen was created specially for this project. The original fireplace had to be retained and it creates a lovely, warm atmosphere.

The use of red creates a cosy atmosphere in this kitchen, with its Viking range cooker.

A CONTEMPORARY LIFESTYLE

IN AN OLD SETTING

A ntiques dealer Kristine Wyffels and her family have created a modern lifestyle in the midst of antiques and decorative objects.

This house was formerly an industrial building, dating back to the eighteenth century. The transformation carried out by Kristine Wyffels illustrates her home-design philosophy: the creation of a dynamic and sober living environment where past and present harmoniously combine. As well as authenticity and quality, the decorative value of the pieces she selects is essential to her: she falls in love with every piece she buys.

Kristine Wyffels did all of the paintwork herself, using paints by Corical and Sherwin Williams.

An oak staircase with a wrought-iron handrail in this hall, painted in Corical lime paints. Linen curtains from the Bruder collection.

A seventeenth-century French cabinet on top of an eighteenth-century Italian console.

This wall is in lime paints based on Sherwin Williams colours. The curtains are in Bruder fabrics. A deep shade of plum as the backdrop for a collection of French moulds from the nineteenth century.

The walls of the living room and the new
shelving units are also in lime paints.

P. 84
The pantry in Corical lime paints in
sophisticated shades of grey.

P. 86 and above
Muted shades of grey for this elegant orangery, painted in lime paints with a colour by Sherwin Williams. An old Swedish table with a cloth in French linen (19th century). An 18th-century Swedish clock and a French refectory table, also from the 18th century.

A Swedish two-section dresser from the eighteenth century, with its original patina.

A SOPHISTICATED

COUNTRY HOUSE

T he famous antiques dealer and decorator Axel Vervoordt designed this new country house in the middle of the woods of Kempen for Eddy Dankers, owner of the painting company Dankers Decor.

The interior was created in close collaboration with the world-famous antiques dealer and is the result of a constant quest for perfection in the use of colour, traditional painting techniques and time-honoured processes.

The walls are in a matte lime-paint finish for a gentle atmosphere. The ceiling is also in lime paint. Floors in Italian nut-wood, *noce bianco*. All of the fabrics were hand-stitched in the studios of May and Axel Vervoordt and made by Dankers Creation. Armchair by Axel Vervoordt. Windows in untreated oak.

In order to create a patina of age, the walls of the orangery were finished in lime paints. The fireplace surround is in tadelakt. The monolithic Pastelone floor is a combination of brick dust and lime: a process that requires a lot of manpower to create the wonderful result.

The walls have a marbled finish. Floor in white Carrara marble, Belgian noir de Mazy marble and a Brèche natural stone.

The kitchen is painted in pale shades of lime paint. Refectory table from Axel Vervoordt. The small 18th-century tiles are a combination of peacock feathers and manganese.

P. 90
The doors and panelling in the dining room are painted with lime paint and casein and decorated with gold edging. The walls are painted in a special Amiata pigment (Italy). A Venetian chandelier in hand-blown glass. The walnut-wood planks are integrated into an oak frame. Silk curtains from the Vervoordt workshops.

An unusual background colour on these shelves: indigo blue, a painter's pigment based on the crocus. Above, gilded leather and a ceiling in grey limewash and casein. The panelling is by Axel Vervoordt.

Walls in a traditional grey-brown finish in this room with its terrazzo floor. Left, a wall painted with pigments based on ox blood.

A subtle harmony of colours in the bathroom: a floor in Carrara marble and Belgian Rouge Royal, a washbasin surround in Rouge Royal, furniture painted in cerulean blue casein and walls in a matte lime finish.

A matte lime finish and marmorino technique for these walls. Authentic eighteenth-century oak doors. The skirting boards are in Rosso di Verona stone, combined with a *trompe-l'œil* section.

Walls in pale cerulean blue.

THE AUTHENTICITY

OF LIME PAINTS

A rte Constructo distributes natural, mineral construction materials made by Unilit (natural hydraulic lime), Coridecor (high-quality finishes based on lime putty) and Keim (silicate paints).

As well as distributing these products, Arte Constructo also advises many architects, professionals and private individuals who wish to restore old (often listed) houses using time-honoured techniques and materials.

In this report, Arte Constructo presents a recent project using lime paints, in collaboration with Dankers Decor painting company.

Hand-coloured lime paints were selected for this country house. A project by Dankers Decor.

P. 98-99
Coridecor offers a wide range of quality mineral products for decoration and finishes. These provide a perfect result on mineral surfaces such as lime-based plasters and old layers of lime paint, brick and porous types of stone. They can be used for both traditional and contemporary interiors. The range includes lime paints and products to create marbled effects, Venetian stucco and smooth, glossy finishes.

TRANSFORMING A CELLAR

INTO A RELAXATION ROOM

A rchitect Bernard De Clerck transformed the semi-subterranean cellar of this country house to create a relaxation room.

The house is on a slope and the owner decided to use this space for relaxation.

He had a swimming pool built outside, and added a sauna, hammam, jacuzzi, fitness centre, sitting area and a summer kitchen inside.

The spacious cellar was converted into a serious of vaulted rooms, separated by walls with arches. The old ceiling beams are still visible.
The whole project was painted with pigmented lime paints in a marbled finish.

The summer kitchen. The sink is in natural Luberon stone and the kitchen work surface is in old oak. The floor is in reclaimed terracotta tommettes. Christine Bekaert designed the lanterns.

The work surface in this kitchen is in old oak. The open fireplace is finished in lime paint. Floor tiles in limestone.

P. 102-103
From the summer sitting room, with the summer kitchen in the background, there is direct access to the fitness room.

The fitness zone with alcoves. The mattresses and cushions are in Indian cotton.

P. 104
The entrance to the jacuzzi. The illuminated niches create a velvet-soft atmosphere, supplemented by natural daylight.

The walls of the shower room are in Moroccan zeliges. Candles in wooden pots.

A DIALOGUE BETWEEN ETHNIC

INSPIRATION AND CONTEMPORARY
ART AND DESIGN

In all of her projects, interior architect Annick Colle likes to creates a confrontation between apparent contradictions.

She cleverly combines antiques from far-off lands with contemporary art and design, creating a very serene atmosphere, where calm and warmth are key.

The project in this report is a convincing illustration of her home-design philosophy.

Annick Colle is the director of a design consultancy and leads a team of interior architects.

Every interior is designed in consultation with the clients and corresponds to modern living requirements.

A pre-Columbian wall hanging from the Nazca region of Peru (ca. 2000 BC). Two armchairs in green buffalo leather beside a wengé table by Christian Liaigre.
In the foreground, two Danish stools designed in 1950 by Paul Hundevad in black leather and palisander, bought from Philippe Denys.
In the background, the dining room with chairs by Hans Wegner.

A calming atmosphere and pale shades in the living room. Photo by Miguel Rio Branco.

A wooden floor in dark-tinted tadelakt. Mirrored cabinets and taps by Dornbracht. The surfaces are in aged Azul Fatima. Cupboards in solid oak, with a brushed and aged finish.

P. 108
The wall units and headboard are in solid, brushed oak with a patinated finish. Bedside table and footstool by Christian Liaigre. On the bed, an African fabric. Reading lamps by S. Davidts.

A Beovision plasma screen by B&O. Parquet in dark-tinted oak. On the left, a work by Jan Decock.

P. 110
Pure white in the light and airy surroundings of this pool house and multifunctional space for teenagers. The red work of art is by Anne Veronica Janssens. B&B seating and a Skipper table in white Carrara marble.

A SYMPHONY IN WHITE

IN AN ANCIENT CASTLE

H endrik Vermoortel and Ingrid Lesage were the impetus behind the transformation of this old castle, parts of which date back to the fourteenth century. The process of turning the building into a modern home took two years.

This listed monument was designed as a cultural enclave: a meeting place where the arts, philosophy, sociology, architecture and conservation will occupy a prominent position.

The interior design is bold: monochrome white in this defiantly contemporary setting.

Contemporary designer furniture on the ground floor: sofas, consoles and cupboards by Ceccotti, red and black armchairs by Le Corbusier for Cassina, Arne Jacobsen Butterfly chairs and lamps by Flos. The oak parquet floor is an original feature.

P. 114-115

The Académie de la Table is one of Ingrid Lesage's initiatives:
part of the castle is set aside for the culinary arts.
The old walls of the castle now have a painted finish.

The private rooms are on the top floor. Monochrome white creates a dramatic look in the living room. Cassina sofas, designed by Starck. Fireplace by De Puydt. Delaere Decor created all of the woodwork, in consultation with architect Hendrik Vermoortel (owner of Buro II). Painting: Kordekor.

An antechamber with two ways through.

CONTEMPORARY STYLE

FOR A NORMANDY-INSPIRED VILLA

C hristine von der Becke renovated this typical Normandy villa in consultation with interior designer Nathalie Van Reeth.

The intention was to retain the charm and style of the original house, not creating a streamlined look, but an interior that perfectly corresponds to modern living requirements. The renovation resulted in a calm and restful atmosphere.

In the living room, old and new harmonise with a few ethnic touches. The floor has a dark finish. The large armchair is upholstered in bright orange velvet.

Style and sophistication in this living room with limewashed walls in a violet shade. The large sofa is upholstered in a dark velvet.

The kitchen floor and surface were created in situ.
The furniture is in pin oak. Black glass cooker hood. The walls in the dining room have gold wallpaper. The chairs are from the 1930s. The consoles come from Hungary. Nathalie Van Reeth chose an original wallpaper for the cloakroom. Washbasin unit in black glass.

Christine von der Becke
designed and created the
bathroom in Emperador natural
stone and stone mosaic tiles.

Custom-made furniture in white-gloss MDF and walnut wood in the parents' bedroom.

The dressing room, designed by Nathalie Van Reeth, is also in white-gloss MDF and walnut wood. The surface of the central unit is in white leather. A custom-made ceiling light.

A paradise in pink for the daughter of the family: pink zelliges in the bathroom and pastel-pink shades for the bedroom.

HOME SERIES

Volume 5 : LIVING WITH COLOUR

The reports in this book are selected from the Beta-Plus collection of home-design books: www.betaplus.com
They have been compiled in a special series by Le Figaro in French language: Ma Déco

Copyright © 2009 Beta-Plus Publishing / Le Figaro
Originally published in French language

PUBLISHER
Beta-Plus Publishing
Termuninck 3
B – 7850 Enghien
Belgium
www.betaplus.com
info@betaplus.com

PHOTOGRAPHY
Jo Pauwels

DESIGN
Polydem - Nathalie Binart

TRANSLATIONS
Laura Watkinson

ISBN: 9789089440365

Printed in China

P. 126-127
An unusual room for a student, created by architect
Stéphane Boens.